MW01488228

The Ingenious Guide to

Pinterest

Steve Eason

Table of Contents

Chapter 3: Following And Unfollowing Others

Chapter 4: Creating and Managing Pinboards

Chapter 8: Viewing and Editing Your Pinterest Activity

Chapter 9: Sharing Pins to Facebook and Twitter

Chapter 10: Protecting Yourself

Conclusion

Introduction

The internet is an ever evolving space that continues to expand in new and interesting ways. It always amazes me when creative ideas, like Pinterest, come out. Once you start using a service like Pinterest, I often wonder why no one ever thought about doing something like that before.

The idea behind Pinterest, is to recreate something like a bulletin board with images and videos that represent your interests and hobbies. Users are able to create individual boards to organize their images or "Pins". These Boards and Pins are then able to be shared with friends.

The development of Pinterest began back in December of 2009 and shortly after it was moved to a closed beta around March of 2010. During this beta period, Ben Silbermann wrote to the site's first 5,000 testers and offered his personal phone number looking for ideas and suggestions. He also personally met with some of its users in order to get feedback. Pinterest continued to operate out of a small apartment until the summer of 2011 with around 10,000 users on the site.

Suddenly, the site was to receive what would be its defining moment. On August 16, 2011, Time Magazine included Pinterest in its list of "50 Best Websites of 2011". It was around this time I started hearing about this new social media site. By December of 2011, the site was listed as one of the top 10 largest social network services with 11 million total visits per week. In January of 2012, it was reported that the site had over 11.7 million unique users, making it the fastest site in history to break through the 10 million user mark.

Since then it has continued to rise to the top of the social media world and in March of 2012 it moved to the third largest social network in the US, passing LinkedIn.

Pinterest was designed from the beginning to be a simple and easy to understand website that was engaging and fun to use. However, even though they have been very successful in accomplishing that goal, one can get overwhelmed and confused with all the options that are available on the site. In writing this book I learned about many features that I didn't know existed.

In this guide I'll show you how to setup your Pinterest account, show you how to use it effectively and how to get the most from the social network site.

Chapter 1: Creating a Pinterest Account
Step 1: Setting it up

When you sign up for a Pinterest account, you can sign up 3 different ways. You can sign up with your Facebook account, Twitter account or just with an email. The primary difference between the options is the ease of logging into your account. You can still connect your Twitter and Facebook accounts to your Pinterest account at a later time, if you choose the email option. Choose whichever option is best for your situation. For all options, in your browser type to start the sign up process.

https://www.pinterest.com/join/signup

Welcome to

Step 1 of 2

Create your account to explore Pinterest.

Connect with

or, sign up with your email address.

Already have an account? Log in.

Signing up with a Facebook account

By signing up with a Facebook account you will automatically tie your new Pinterest account to your Facebook account. This will allow you to share your Pinterest activity on your Facebook timeline, should you choose to do so. If you don't already have a Facebook account, you will have to create one before continuing. To sign up for Pinterest, click on Connect with Facebook.

Once you do this, the browser will load your Facebook account, in which you must login if you aren't already. Once you log in you will be prompted to allow the Pinterest app to have access to your Facebook account. Click on Add to Facebook to continue the login process.

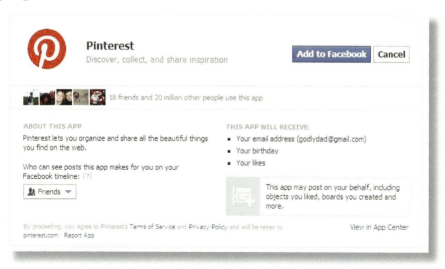

On this next screen, you will create your new Pinterest account that links to your Facebook account. Complete the forms provided, entering the user name you would like, your email address and a password. Click **Create Account**.

Signing up with a Twitter Account

By signing up with a Twitter account, you will automatically tie your new Pinterest account to your Twitter account. This will allow you to share your Pinterest activity on your Twitter account, should you choose to do so. If you don't already have a Twitter account, you will have to create one before continuing. To sign up for Pinterest, click on **Connect with Twitter**.

Once you do this, the browser will open the Twitter authorization window, where you authorize Pinterest and Twitter to communicate with each other. You will have to log into your Twitter account if you aren't already. Once you have entered your login information, click on **Sign in**.

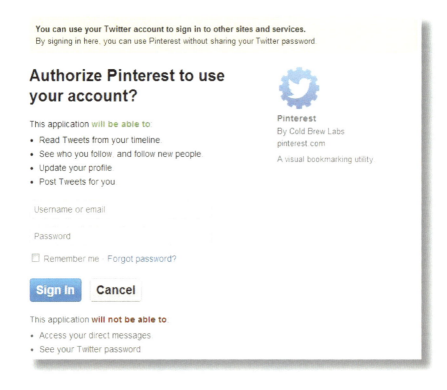

On this next screen, you will create your new Pinterest account that links to your Twitter account. Complete the forms provided, entering the user name you would like, your email address and a password. Click **Create Account**.

Signing up with an email address

By signing up with just an email address, you can keep your Pinterest account separate from your Twitter or Facebook accounts. This is also useful if you don't have either of those accounts. You can add connectivity to both a Twitter and Facebook account at a later time if you choose.

On the same screen where you start the process of creating an account through Facebook or Twitter, just below those buttons you will see an option that says, "**or, sign up with your email address.**" Click on this link to continue.

Once you do this, you will be taken to the Create Your Account page. Complete the forms provided, entering the user name you would like, your email address, password and your first and last name. Click **Create Account**.

Note about your name: The name that you enter in the First and Last name fields will be displayed on every pin and comment you make. There are no restrictions on what you can enter into these fields.

Create your account

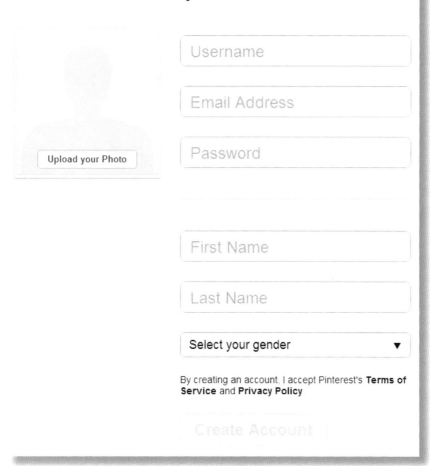

Upload your Photo

Username

Email Address

Password

First Name

Last Name

Select your gender ▼

By creating an account, I accept Pinterest's **Terms of Service** and **Privacy Policy**

Create Account

Pinterest Business Accounts

If you are planning on using Pinterest as a business, I recommend you sign up for a business Pinterest account. The business account allows you to use your business name instead of an individual, plus they are going to be adding new features that will be useful for businesses in the future.

Visit this URL to start the process for creating a business Pinterest account.

http://business.pinterest.com/

Your user name will be a part of the URL for your Pinterest Page. So if your user name is "WholeFoods", your URL will be http://www.pinterest.com/wholefoods. Your user name and first and last name can be different.

PROFILE INFO (shown publicly)

Business Name	Ingenious Internet Income	How you'll appear on Pinterest
Username	http://pinterest.com/ IngeniousIncome	

Image

Upload an Image

Refresh from Facebook

Refresh from Twitter

About

Steve Eason is a professional blogger
(http://www.ingeniousinternetincome.com

Pinterest Welcome Screen

Once you have completed signing up, you will be taken to the Pinterest Welcome screen. On this page you will choose an image of something that you like. Pinterest will give you several options to choose from and you have to select 5 different images in order to proceed. You will be setup automatically to follow those pinners, which will show on your home page once you log in. You can remove these from your account at anytime. Pinterest is providing you with some images to get you started.

Once this is complete, you will be taken to your Pinterest Home page. You will receive a message across the top of the screen, asking you to verify your email address.

Check your email account and look for the email from Pinterest. Click on the button to **Verify your email address with Pinterest.** This will open your home page on Pinterest in your browser.

At the top right hand corner of the page, click on **your name** to open your Pinterest profile page. Once the profile page loads, on the right hand side, in the middle of the page you will see a number of the people you are following. (ie. 57 following). Click on this area to open the following view.

On this page you can quickly see all the people that you are following. Pinterest sets up several popular pinners so that you can get an idea of how Pinterest works. This page will give you a chance to remove any or all of those that you are following if you prefer. Just click on the **Unfollow button** that is next to their information (it's grayed out initially).

Logging In and out of Pinterest

Now that you have an account set up, you can log into your account, if you aren't already. The login process can be a little confusing the first time you do it. Go to **http://www.pinterest. com**. If you aren't logged in, you will have a yellow box with the option to Login on it. Click **Login**.

The Pinterest login page will come up with 3 options for logging in; **Facebook, Twitter and Email**.

Logging in with email

If you created your account using an email address, enter that same email address in the box provided. Type in your password and click **Login**. You should be taken to your Pinterest home page.

Logging in with Facebook

If you created your account using a Facebook account, click on **Login with Facebook**. This takes you to a Facebook login page. Enter your Facebook email address and password and click **Log in**. You should then be taken to your Pinterest home page.

Logging in with Twitter

If you created your account using a Twitter account, click on **Login with Twitter**. This takes you to a Twitter login page. Enter your Twitter email account or username and password and click **Sign in**. You should then be taken to your Pinterest home page.

TIPS:

When I clicked Login with Facebook, Pinterest logged me in immediately. I didn't have to enter my information. Why did this happen?

If you are already logged into your Facebook account in the browser you are using, then Pinterest automatically recognizes this information and uses it. This will also happen if you chose to login with a Twitter account.

Do I have to use the same email account for Pinterest that I used for Twitter or Facebook?

No, you can use different email addresses for each service. They don't have to be the same.

Understanding the Pinterest interface

Pinterest was designed to be easily navigated and intuitive. The primary focus on your Pinterest account will be the images. Across the top of the page, you will find the menu where you can access just about everything you will need when using Pinterest.

On the far left of the page, is a search box. On the far right are 3 options; Add (add a pin), About (Information about Pinterest) and your Name with your profile image.

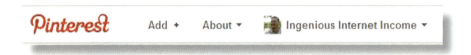

Clicking on the **Add +** button opens the Add a Pin window. Hovering over the **About** item will open up a menu showing additional options available to you in relation to Pinterest. Hovering over your name, will open a menu showing you options available concerning your account. If you click on your name, it will open your personal profile page.

In the middle of the menu area, is the primary way you will navigate through the Pinterest site. The default options are; Following, Categories, Everything, Popular and Gifts.

Following – Your page loads showing pins from the people you are following by default. Clicking on this option when viewing the page, will refresh the page. Clicking on the page when on another page, you will be brought back here.

Categories – When you hover over this menu item, the listing of available Categories will be displayed. If you click on any category, you will be taken to the latest pins that are organized under that category. Clicking on the word **Category**, will open up a page where you can get a preview of the pins under each category.

Everything – As the name implies, this is everything. When clicking on this menu option, it opens the page that will show you everything that has been posted last. If you click on this menu option while viewing the Everything page, it will refresh the page, showing anything that has been added recently.

Popular – When you click on this menu item, you will see the recent pins that are the most popular with Pinterest users. Typically this will be items that are being repined and commented on the most.

Gifts – When you hover over this menu item, it will display a menu with different price ranges. We will talk a little more about adding prices to your pins a little later, but this menu allows you to see any pins that have prices on them, based on their values. Clicking on the main menu item, **Gifts**, will show you everything that has a price with no filters. The idea behind this category is to give you ideas for gifts based on your particular price range.

Recent Activity and Scroll To Top

When on your home page, which you can get back to by clicking on the Pinterest Logo at the top of the page, you will see on the left side of the screen at box with the title of Recent Activity. In this box, you will see updates on what has happened recently with your pins and pinboards.

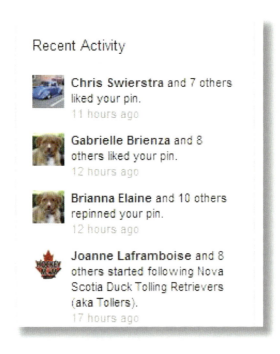

As you scroll down the page, one thing you will notice is that the menus will move off the page out of sight. You will be scrolling a lot when using Pinterest, so it is helpful to know that once the menu leaves the visible area, you will have a button come up on the bottom right corner that says Scroll To Top. By clicking on this button, you will be taken back to the top of the page.

Chapter 2: Setting Up Your Profile

Now that you have created your account on Pinterest, you should take a few minutes to update and customize your Bio. Your bio is a place where you can tell other members what you are interested in and a little bit of information about yourself. You can also add your location and a link to your website, should you choose. This information is publically available, so be sure not to post anything that you don't mind the world knowing.

Editing Your Bio

When you are logged into Pinterest, click on your name at the top right part of the screen. This will bring up your Bio page. Just under your name, there is a box where you can add a short description. Just click in that area to start typing. Once you have finished, click **Save Description**.

Add Your Website

The globe icon just below your description is where you click to add your website or blog. Click the Globe icon and a box appears with a check mark next to it. Type in your website address and click the check mark to confirm the address.

Add Your Location

Next to that box is a Map pin. Click this box and type in the name of your location in the blank area. Click the check box to confirm your location.

Editing Your Profile In The Future

Later on you are able to come back to this page and edit your profile as needed. However, in order to edit some of these fields you will have to click on the **Edit Profile** button in the middle of the page.

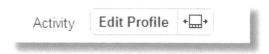

Adding A Profile Image

It's a good idea to add a Profile image to your Bio page so that visitors can get a sense of who you are. If you used Facebook or Twitter to sign up for Pinterest, your profile image from those services will have been imported by default. You can change this image to another image if you choose.

On the Pinterest home page, click on your name, which takes you to your profile page. Click on **Edit Profile**, in the middle of the page. Just below your name on your profile page, you will have an option to upload an image. If you created your account through email, you will have a large red picture with a white pin in the middle as your profile image. If you used Facebook or Twitter to sign up, it will have your profile image here.

Click on **Upload an Image** to choose a new picture from your computer. The button changes to a box with a browse button. Use this button to choose a new image from your computer. Once you have identified an image to use, click **Open**.

The image will be uploaded and added to the box. Scroll to the bottom of this page, and click **Save Profile** to save your changes.

If you change your image on Facebook or Twitter, you can also click on the buttons labeled "Refresh from Facebook" or "Refresh from Twitter" to update your Pinterest image to match.

TIPS:

Pinterest will attempt to scale your image to fit the available space on your profile image once you save the profile. If it doesn't scale properly, you might have to choose a larger image.

Remember that the image is square in shape, so if you want to control how the image is displayed, it's best to edit the image in a graphics program such as Paint, before uploading it to Pinterest.

Edit Account Settings

We've already seen a few settings available on the Edit Account Setting page, but let's look at the remaining options.

On this page, you can change the email address and password on your account. You can also change the language and gender if needed. Your profile's First name and Last name is able to be edited on this page as is your user name.

We've already discussed how you can upload and change your profile image here. You can also change your About information (Bio), your location and your website.

You can also link your Facebook and Twitter accounts here, if you had not already done so when you created your account. Just be sure to click **Save Profile** once you have made your changes or corrections.

Finding Help

Even though the site is designed to be easy to understand and navigate, there will be times when you need some extra help finding a feature or changing a setting. The help area for Pinterest can be found by hovering over the **About** menu item on the right side of the screen and then selecting **Help**. There is lots of useful information in the Help section should you need it.

Installing A Bookmarklet

The idea behind Pinterest is for you to use the site to collect and display images that you find when you are looking up information online. In order to make this process even easier, you can install what is known as a **bookmarklet** in your web browser to make it easier to pin as you surf.

To create this bookmarklet in Google Chrome and Mozilla Firefox, it's as easy as dragging it to your bookmark bar. To do this, go to the following page: **http://www.pinterest.com/about/goodies**

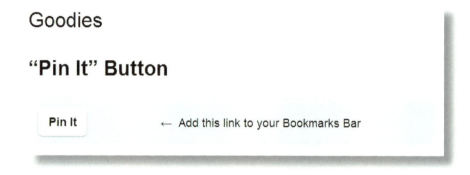

Right at the top of the page, you will find a large **Pin it button**. Just simply drag this button to your bookmarks bar in either browser to install it for future use.

If you want to install this button in Internet Explorer, the process is a little different. You still go to the same page, **http://www. pinterest.com/about/goodies** to access the pin.

Right click on the pin button and choose **Add to Favorites**. A window will come up asking where you want to add the favorite. Select **Favorites bar** from the drop-down list and click **Add**.

Browsing the Pinterest Home page

When you come to the Pinterest Home page, by default it will be displaying pins from Pinners that you are following. They are sorted with the most recent at the top of the page moving down to the less recent as you scroll down. The more people you are following, the more variety you will find on this page.

If you are not logged into your Pinterest account or you don't have an account, the Everything Page will be displayed by default instead.

Browsing the Pinterest Everything Page

The Everything page shows all the latest pins without any filtering. If you want to go to this page directly, you can type in your browser: **http://www.pinterest.com/all**

Browsing the Pinterest Popular

If you click on the **Popular** menu item, the view will change to display the latest popular images. These are the images that are being repinned and commented on the most.

Browsing the Pinterest Categories

If you want to narrow down the pins that are shown, you can choose a particular category by hovering over the Categories menu item and then selecting which category to view. The images displayed will change to those that are marked in the category you choose.

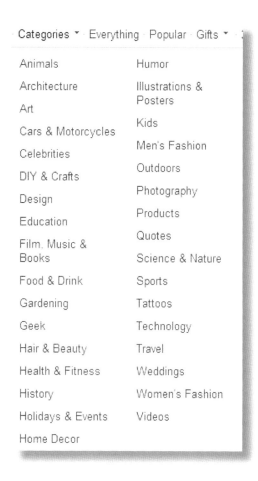

Finding Pins with Pinterest Search

The above options are great for finding images when you don't have a particular topic in mind. It's a lot of fun to just scroll through each of the categories and popular results, repinning those images that speak to you. But when you want to find images based on a particular topic or idea, the Pinterest search box is your best option.

Found at the top left side of the page, you can simply type in a word or words in the search box and Pinterest will create a feed based on your search terms. It will also generate lists of Boards and Pinners that match your keyword search. Once your search results are displayed, at the top of the page you will find the words Boards and Pinners. Click on either one of those options to see those results.

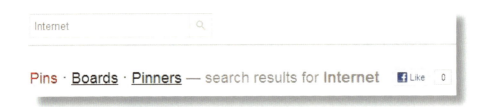

Viewing a Pin

Viewing a Pin in Pinterest is intuitive. Just click on any image that interests you. This will enlarge the image, centering it on your page. When in this view, you will find some additional information provided for this particular pin.

At the top of the pin, is the name of the user who posted the pin along with their profile image. It also tells you how long ago the pin was added and where it came from. If the pin was uploaded by the user, it will state that the image was uploaded by them. On the right side of the top portion of the screen is a button that you can click on to follow that user. Keep in mind that this **Follow** button will add this entire users account to your follow list. Not just this image or board.

You'll also note that if a price was entered into the comment area, the pin will automatically display the price tag over the top left corner of the pin. This also automatically adds the pin to the gifts tab.

On the right side of the image, you will find social sharing buttons. These buttons allow you to share this image with your Facebook friends or Twitter followers.

Below these options is an **Embed** button. You can use this button to add this image to your website.

Below that is a **Report pin** button. If you feel this image is inappropriate, click this button to report the image to Pinterest.

If you wish you email this image to someone or yourself, click the last button, @ Email. When you click this button a form will appear allowing you to enter the name and email address where you want to send it, along with a short message.

Below the image is where you will find any comments that have been made about this image. You can also add additional comments here. To the right of the comments you will see a little square icon that is the report button. If you feel the comment is inappropriate, you can report the comment by clicking on this icon.

Below the comment area is the Pin's board summary. This shows you preview images of pins that are found in the same Pinboard that the original image is found. If you like what you see in this Pinboard and want to follow the whole board, you can click on the **Follow** button in this area to follow just this board. If you choose to do this, you will not be following every board that the original Pinner has, but just this specific Pinboard.

Further down you will find a summary of the original pinner of the image. This area has a **Follow** button if you wish to follow this user. It could be different from the user who's pin you are viewing. Additionally this area also show you where the source was for the original image. This is where the person found the original image, if they didn't upload it themselves.

If the image has been repinned, below this area you will find a summary of the users who repinned the image. It will display the number of users who repinned the image, thumbnails of those users profiles and an option to look at the other users not included in the summary. Below this you will find a quick summary of users who liked the pin. Below this you will find a quick summary of users who liked the pin.

Reporting A Pin

As mentioned earlier, when you are viewing a pin, on the right side of the image, is a button for reporting a pin. When you click on the **Report Pin** button, a new window will appear asking you to choose a reason why you are reporting the pin. Click on a reason why you are reporting the pin and then click on **Report Pin**. The window will change to a thank you box and then disappears.

Report Pin

Why are you reporting this pin?

○ Nudity or Pornography

○ Attacks a group or individual

○ Graphic Violence

○ Hateful Speech or Symbols

○ Actively promotes self-harm

○ Spam

○ Other

Report Pin   **Is this your intellectual property?**

Chapter 3: Following And Unfollowing Others

What is Following?

One of the unique features in Pinterest is how you are able to create your own customized feed by following other users. When you log into Pinterest, your default view is pins that have been pinned by users that you follow. Following is essentially including a user or a particular board in your feed so that you see any updates that are made to that board.

You can follow anyone you wish without having to get permission from that user. You could choose to follow someone who is interested in topics that you are interested in or you could choose someone with completely different tastes. It's all up to you who you wish to follow.

Follow a Pinner

If you find someone you are interested in following, click on their name under one of their recent pins. This opens up the user's page, where you will see all their boards. Decide if you want to follow just one of their boards or all of them. If you decide to follow all of their boards, click the **Follow All** button at the top of the page.

Click on your name at the top of the page and on your profile page, click on **Following** to see a listing of all the users you are following. You can then confirm that the new person you are following shows up.

Follow a Board

If you decide that you don't want to follow all the boards of a particular user, you can choose just to follow one of their boards. This is extremely useful when you find someone who likes the same cars you do, but also likes clowns and you don't. In this case you can follow their cars board and leave the clowns board off your list.

This is just as easy to accomplish. Find the board that you want to follow, and click the board name to open it up. Click the **Follow** button near the top of the page and the button will change to a grayed out **Unfollow**.

Again you can go to your profile page and click on **Following** to confirm that the board was added. You will notice that when you see boards listed on your Following page, there will be a Follow button next to the users name, so that you can follow all their boards if you wish.

Repin a Pin

Most often you will find yourself scanning through categories or the everything page and pinning individual images to your boards. This is referred to as repinning. Repinning is pinning content already in Pinterest to one of your boards.

When you pin content from other websites online, that is called pinning. Any image that you have already pinned on one of your boards can be repinned to another board should you choose. You are not restricted to placing the image on only one board.

To Repin a pin you can just hover over the image and three options will come up over the top of the image. **Repin, Like and Comment**. Click on **Repin** and the repin window comes up. Below the image is a drop down box where you can choose an existing board to pin the image to or you can choose to create a new board. You create the new board by scrolling down to the bottom of that selection box and entering in the name of the new board. After it is pinned you will see a confirmation message appear.

Like a Pin

When you hover over an image as we mentioned earlier, you will also see a box that allows you to like the pin. You can "like" an image without pinning it to one of your boards.

To Like a pin, just hover over the image and click on the **Like** button. The button changes to a grayed out **Unlike** once it's clicked. If you click the button a second time, it will change back to **Like**. This is unliking the pin, thus reversing your Like action.

Keep in mind this is different than Liking the image on Facebook. To like the image on Facebook, click on the image to bring it up full page. On the right side of the image is a **Facebook Like** button. If you click this button, you will be prompted to login to Facebook if you aren't already.

Once you have liked a few pins, you can find the list of images you liked on your profile menu. Hover over your name and a menu will appear. On that menu is one option listed as **Likes**. Clicking on this option will display all the images you have liked.

Comment on a Pin

You can also add a comment to any pin you come across. To add a comment, hover over the image and click on the **Comment** button. This will open a comment box just under the image. Type in your comment and once you are finished, click on the **Comment** button to save it.

If you want to view the comments you've made in the past, you can find these listed on your Activity page. Click on your name to open your profile page. On the menu bar, you will see a menu option labeled **Activity**. Click on this to display your recent activity, including comments.

Deleting a Comment

If you decide you want to remove a comment from a pin, you can always delete it. You are unable to edit comments, but you can delete it and add a new one. To delete a comment, find the comment through your activity page or by clicking on the pin. Scroll down to your comment and click the **X** next to your comment to remove it.

Viewing the Source of a Pin

If an image was added from an external website and not repinned from Pinterest, you can view the original source of the image. In almost all cases, the original website information is added to the pin automatically when it's added to Pinterest. All you have to do is click on the image to see that original source.

If the image was added by a user who uploaded it from their computer, it will not have the information added automatically. The user has to manually add any information to the image at that time. Frequently, this is not done by the original user.

Chapter 4: Creating and Managing Pinboards

What is a Pinboard?

A pinboard or a board is essentially a storage location for your pins. It's an easy way to organize the images you have pinned. You can name the boards whatever you'd like to name them, rearrange them however you feel like, choose an image to be the cover image and you can even have guests pin new content to your boards. You could think about it like you would a bulletin board you might have at home. You might organize items on your board based on categories, individuals or maybe recipes you want to make. You can have multiple boards so use them to organize your pins in ways that makes sense to you.

Viewing Pinboards

To view your pinboards, you can either click on your name or hover over your name and click on **Boards** on the menu. This will bring up all the boards you have created. The boards will list how many pins are in each board and will display a preview of the last 4 pins that were added and the cover image for the board.

To view other users boards, click on the users name and it will display the boards that that user has created, in the same format that you see on your board list.

Creating New Pinboards

You have to have at least one pinboard at all times. There are several ways you can new boards to your profile.

One way to create new boards is by clicking on the **Add+** link at the top of the page. This will bring up a window where you can choose to create a new pin or board. Click on **Board** to create a new board. The next window will have you enter in information for this new board.

On the new window, type in a board name and choose which category you feel this board fits into. The next option is to choose if you want this board to be a secret board or not. You can only create **3 secret boards** on your account, so consider this option carefully.

You can then choose if you want to add any other users to have the ability to pin to this board. Just type in the first and last name of the user and Pinterest will display any users with that name for you to choose. After selecting a user, just click **Invite** to add them to the board.

Once you are finished, click on **Create Board** to finish.

Secret Boards

Secret boards were created to allow you the ability to create boards that would not be visible through the following menu options: category sections, Popular, Everything, anyone's search results, your follower's feed, your own home feed, or even pins or activity pages on your profile. An example of a board you would want to make a secret board would be something like a family event you wanted to keep private but allow specific people to view.

You cannot change an existing board to a secret board. However a secret board can be changed to a viewable board at any point in the future.

Note: If you change a secret board to public, then it cannot be changed back to a secret board.

You can add additional users to a secret board so that they can see the board. However, only the board's creator can make the secret board viewable to everyone. Any people that are invited to view the board, can request to add additional people to the board, but the creator has to approve them prior to them having access. When a new user is added to a secret board, they can repin and like pins on the board.

Note: All contributors can repin the contents of the secret board to other boards. Those repins will not display any information about the secret board or link back to that board, but those images can be seen by anyone viewing that other board.

Editing and Deleting Pinboards

If you want to make any changes or want to remove a board, click on the board you want to change. In the middle of the page you'll find a button labeled **Edit Board**. Click that button to open up the options that you can change on that board.

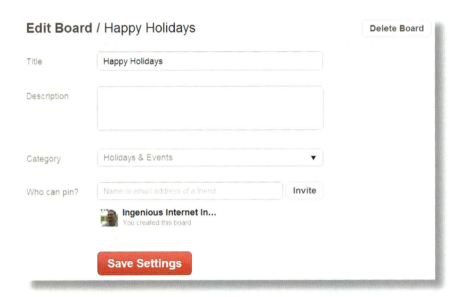

On the options page, you have the ability to change the Title, Description, Category and who can pin to that board. Just make any changes you want to make and then click **Save Settings**.

If you want to delete the board completely, click the **Delete Board** button located on the top right side of the page. You will receive a confirmation message before the board is deleted.

Rearranging Pinboards

You do have the ability to rearrange your Pinboards in any order you would like them displayed. You don't have to leave them how they were created originally. By default the boards are displayed in the order that they were created. You can rearrange them by categories, alphabetically or whatever makes the most sense.

It's easy to move them around, however the button to enable this feature is a little hard to spot if you don't know what you're looking for.

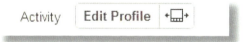

When you click on your name and go to your profile page, you will see a button in the middle of the screen just to the right of the **Edit Profile** button. It's an image of a board with arrows pointing to the right and left. When you hover over this button it will display a popup name; **Rearrange Boards**. Click on this button to enable the ability to drag your boards around. Once you are finished, click the Red Checkbox to confirm your changes.

Tips:

You have to move the boards one at a time and cannot rearrange them by groups. Depending on the number of boards you have this could become quite a chore. It's a good idea to create a board plan prior to creating a large number of boards and we'll talk about that a little later in this guide.

Also note the way that the boards move around. When you drag a board up to another row, the last board on that row will automatically slide down to the row below it. This can help you figure out how to move the boards around.

Moving a Pin to Another Pinboard

Inevitably you are going to come across a time when you want to move a pin to another board. If you accidentally add the pin to the wrong board or need to split up images on a board, it's fairly easy to move it to another board.

Click in the board name or the cover image to open that board. Find the image you want to move to another board. When you hover over the image, click on the **Edit** button to show the Edit window. On this window, there is a drop down box labeled **Board**, where you can change which board you want this pin to be located on. Once you choose the new board location where you want this pin to be, click on **Save Pin** to confirm your changes.

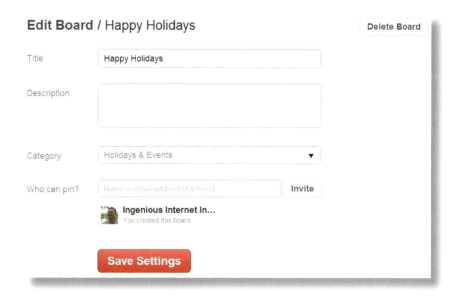

What if I want to move the pin to two different boards?

You can only move a pin to a single board, however you can repin that image on another board by clicking on the **Repin** button when you hover over the image. By repining the image, you will add it to another board while keeping the original image where it was before.

Editing Pins on a Pinboard

If you want to make changes to any of your pins, you can do that by hovering over the pin and clicking on the Edit button. On the Edit page, you can change the description, the URL that the image links to or the board that it's located on. Once you make any changes, click **Save Pin** to commit those changes.

Deleting Pins on a Pinboard

If you change your mind about adding a particular pin or you added multiple copies of a pin, you can delete the pin from your board. To do this, hover over the image and click on the **Edit** button when it appears.

On the edit page, click on the **Delete Pin** button located on the right side. A confirmation window will appear giving you chance to cancel the action before the image is removed.

Note: When deleting a pin, it will be removed from your account permanently. You cannot keep pins on your account without them being located on a board. If you don't want to delete the pin completely, some people setup an alternate board named something like **Temporary** or **Under Review** to place those images in. You can also click on **Like** for that image and then you will be able to find the image again by reviewing your Likes.

Selecting a Cover for a Board

The large image attributed to each board, is called the Cover image. By default, this image will be the last image you added to that board. But you can control which image is used as the cover image. By choosing a good image for your board, you can help visitors easily understand what your board is about. Placing a really good image will also attract new viewers to your board.

There are two ways to set the cover image. The first way is to hover over the board when viewing your profile and a button will appear labeled **Edit Board Cover**. Click on this button to open the cover image edit window.

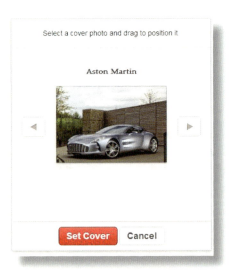

This will display the current image in the middle of the screen with arrows on both sides of the image, which allows you to scroll between the available images to choose from. Scroll back and forth to identify an image you want to use for your cover photo.

You will notice that a rectangle is covering a portion of the image, so that you can see how it's going to appear as the cover image. Once you decide which image you want to use, you can move the image behind this rectangle to line it up properly. When you are happy with the results, click on Set Cover to save your changes.

The second way to change the cover image is inside the board itself. Click on the board's current cover image or name to open up the board. When viewing your board pins, as you hover over any image on that board, a button will appear over the image labeled Set Board Cover. Click on the button to open the cover image editor.

This will display the current image in the middle of the screen with arrows on both sides of the image, which allows you to scroll between the available images to choose from. Scroll back and forth to identify an image you want to use for your cover photo.

You will notice that a rectangle is covering a portion of the image, so that you can see how it's going to appear as the cover image. Once you decide which image you want to use, you can move the image behind this rectangle to line it up properly. When you are happy with the results, click on Set Cover to save your changes.

Chapter 5: Pinning to Pinterest

Understanding Pins

A Pin is what Pinterest is all about. Essentially a Pin is an image or video that you find interesting or worthy of adding to your account for one reason or another. You then can organize your pins into categories, use it to plan activities or just pins that catch your attention. You can add pins to your account through a variety of ways.

Pinning From Pinterest

Pinning from within Pinterest starts by pressing the **Add +** button at the top of the page. When you click on this button, you will see the Add window come up. On this window you can either Add a pin using a URL or web address, Upload a pin from your computer or Create a new board.

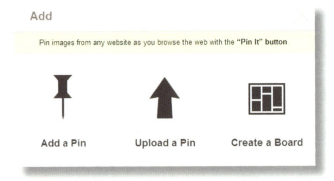

Add a Pin – If you click **Add a Pin**, you will be asked for a URL address to find images on that website. Just enter in a web address including the http:// and then click on **Find Images**. A new window will come up showing you the images that it found on that particular website. You are able to scroll through the images on the left hand side of that window.

On the right side, you can choose which board you want to add the new Pin to. You can also create a new board by scrolling to the bottom of the board listing and then entering a new name for the new board. Enter a description for the pin and if you want to share the pin, check the box and click **Pin it**.

Upload a Pin – If you wish to upload an image, click on **Upload a Pin**. This will bring up a new window where you can choose a file from your computer to upload to Pinterest. Select the image you wish to add, choose a category to add it to, describe the pin, check the box if you wish to share the pin and then click on **Pin it** once you are finished. As with adding a pin, you can create a new board by scrolling to the end of the board listing on the drop down box.

Create a Board – You can create a new board by clicking the **Create a board** button. On the new window, type in a board name and choose which category you feel this board fits into. The next option is to choose if you want this board to be a secret board or not.

You can then choose if you want to add any other users to have the ability to pin to this board. Just type in the first and last name of the user and Pinterest will display any users with that name for you to choose. After selecting a user, just click **Invite** to add them to the board.

Once you are finished, click on **Create Board** to finish.

Pinning from your Browser

The idea behind Pinterest is for you to use the site to collect and display images that you find when you are looking up information online. In order to make this process even easier, you can install what is known as a **bookmarklet** in your web browser to make it easier to pin as you surf.

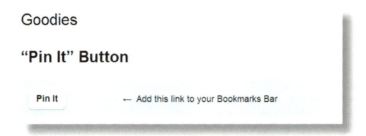

To create this bookmarklet in Google Chrome and Mozilla Firefox, it's as easy as dragging it to your bookmark bar. To do this, go to the following page: **http://www.pinterest.com/about/goodies**. Right at the top of the page, you will find a large **Pin it** button. Just simply drag this button to your bookmarks bar in either browser to install it for future use.

If you want to install this button in Internet Explorer, the process is a little different. You still go to the same page, **http://www.pinterest.com/about/goodies** to access the pin. Right click on the pin button and choose Add to Favorites. A window will come up asking where you want to add the favorite. Select **Favorites bar** from the drop-down list and click **Add**.

Once you have this button, just click on it from any website to start the process of pinning an image to your Pinterest Account.

Using the Pin it Button on Websites

Some websites will provide you a button to simplify the process of adding images from that site to Pinterest. To use this button, just click on it to start the process.

A new window will open allowing you to select which image on that page you want to pin. Once you selected the image, choose which board you wish to add this new image to and enter in a description. If you wish to share this new pin, check the box next to Facebook and/or Twitter and click **Pin It**.

The success window will come up next, where you can choose to see the new pin on Pinterest, Tweet it on Twitter or Share it on Facebook.

Pinning and Playing Videos

The great thing about Pinterest is that it's not just about images. You can add videos to your boards, too. You could add tutorial videos to your craft boards, or music videos to band boards or demonstrations to other boards. You can also view other videos uploaded by users under the category menu. You'll recognize a pinned video by the play button in the middle of the image. When you view a video that has been pinned to Pinterest directly on the board it's located in.

25% off discount and How to Build a Blog in Less than 4 Minutes and Write Your First Blog Post

by TheIngeniousIncome

youtube.com

Pinning a video

Pinning a video is just as easy as it is to add an image to your boards. Click the **Add +** button at the top of the page. When you click on this button, you will see the Add window come up. On this window click on **Add a pin** where you will be asked for a URL address to find a video on that website. You will be shown the video that is able to be pinned. Choose the category to add the pin to, enter a description, choose if you want to share it and then click **Pin It**.

You can also use your Bookmarklet to add the video to Pinterest. When you click the button it will bring up a new window where you can choose the video you want to add to Pinterest. On the next page, choose the board you want to add the video to, add a description, choose to share if you wish and then click **Pin It** to finish.

Viewing Pinned Videos

Viewing videos on Pinterest is as easy as clicking on the pin to open it up full screen. When the new window opens, the video should start playing automatically. When the video is playing, you can pause and resume the video using the controls that are located at the bottom of the video. You can also adjust the quality of the video just like you would if viewing the video at its original source.

Browsing and Searching for Videos on Pinterest

You can browse the most recently pinned videos on Pinterest very easily. To show only videos, hover over Categories in the middle of the tool bar and then select **Videos** on the menu that appears. This will display only videos that have been added to Pinterest.

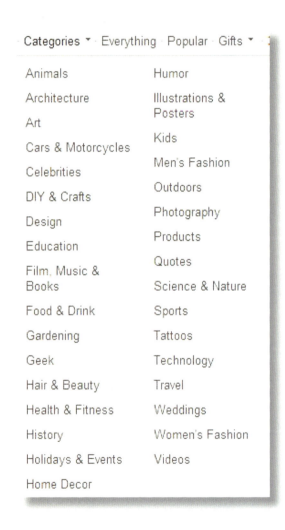

At this time, you cannot search specifically in the Category of Videos. You can search for your keyword with the word video or videos added to it and sometimes you will get what you are looking for. This depends greatly on the description added by the pinner. An example would be, searching for "Charlie Brown video".

Chapter 6: Finding Interesting Things To Pin

Once you've setup your account, played around with creating boards and are ready to start adding content, inevitably the question comes up on what you should pin. Everyone is different and they have different ideas of what is interesting and worth pinning. The best way to approach this at first, is to pin what you find interesting and worth sharing with others. Let's look a little further at what makes a good pin.

What and Why do people Pin?

As you start browsing through the pins that have been added recently, you'll start to get an idea of what people are pinning. What I find interesting is looking at some of the statistics and seeing what really is being shared on Pinterest.

Repinning is King

More than 80% of the pins added to Pinterest are actually repins. Meaning they are already on Pinterest and being repinned on other boards. So that would also mean that only 20% of pins are new images from sources outside of Pinterest.

The Most Popular Pins Are From Etsy.com

One of the largest sources for new pins, comes from Etsy.com. Etsy is an online site that allows members to sell craft projects that they make or design. It makes a lot of sense why this site is one of the biggest sources of images.

Most Popular Categories are...

Home   (17%)
Arts and Crafts   (12%)
Style/Fashion   (11%)
Food   (10%)

Why are they pinning what they pin?

Most of the time people are pinning images that relate to products that they are selling or have created. Pinterest has become a major resource for getting products in front of people and more businesses are turning to the site for this reason. However, the other major reasons people pin images would be to laugh, to remember, to share with others who enjoy that topic or subject and to create lists of things that they want or would love to have.

For example, I have a board with cars I'd love to drive. A family member of mine has a board with fashion ideas that she refers back to when she needs ideas. Another family member has a board with food ideas and recipes to try later.

Recommendations for Pinning

Pinning Visually Interesting Items

If you want your pins to be repinned, posting visually interesting items is a great way to get that accomplished. Remember that Pinterest is a visual social network and the image is everything. You want to pin images that capture the attention of visitors who are browsing through the boards.

Images with bold colors or stark contrasts will often stand out among the other images around it. Unusual images or outlandish photos are also good for pinning. Anything that is likely to draw attention. It's also good to post images that have a single item against a plain background. That helps it to stand out.

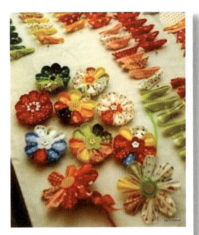

Rox's world of quilts: How to make a kanzashi flower

Pinning Text

You can't pin just text in Pinterest, however you can pin images that include text in them. Just spend a few minutes looking through the pins already posted and you'll see all kinds of text images already pinned.

Converting text into visual images is more than just typing text and saving a screen shot of it. You need to add flair and some creativity. Many of these images will include historical quotes, encouragement or humorous thoughts surrounded by a design that ties in with the theme. For example, a quote about a beach might be written in the sand with a finger. It's about being creative with the message that captures the attention of the viewer.

Humor in Pinning

Humor always works with this type of social site. Humor with animals is even better. Humorous images usually do really well on Pinterest because they get shared a lot. Even text with funny quotes get spread around quite a bit. Find an image with a funny situation, add a great comment and it's likely to spread like wildfire, if it's good. The idea is to create something that others can identify with. An image with a cat stuck in a milk carton with the caption "Monday's are the worst" would likely be very popular. Just think outside of the box.

Lifestyle Pinning

As we already mentioned earlier, the popular categories for pinning all really relate to our lifestyles, which can become great images to share. Think about sharing great pictures of home designs, fashion designs and accessories, food and art. I can't tell you how many images I've come across just showing how to create a great outfit for a night out or how to decorate your mantle for the holidays. If it's about creating there are likely others who can relate and will appreciate what you have to share.

holiday mantle
1 repin

Travel and Bucket List Pins

Another extremely popular topic to pin about is travel and bucket list subjects. It's a lot of fun to create a board about where you want to travel to and add all kinds of images about those locations. Create a board for each country you want to visit and add images of places you want to go, and then when you are able to visit you'll have your itinerary all ready to go.

Bucket lists are collections of things you want to do, places you want to go or things you want to eat before you die. These boards can have just about anything you can think of in them, but they have a purpose and a meaning behind them. Even better, create a To do Bucket List and a Completed Bucket List and move those pins you've completed over once you completed them. It's great inspiration to get out there and explore.

Gift Pinning

You can use your boards to collect ideas for gifts; for you or for others. If you create a board for you, you could then share that board with friends and family so that they can get some ideas when it comes time to shop for a gift for you. It's like your own personal registry.

If you create boards for others, you can always add to it as you learn more about others and when it's time to find a gift for them, you'll have all kinds of ideas to pick from.

So you can see, Pinterest can be used in so many different ways and there are plenty of other ideas out there. Hopefully these will help you get started and you can go from there. Be creative and explore. Don't limit yourself based on what other people are doing.

Chapter 7: Hashtags and Mentions

Hashtags and Mentions are important to utilize when writing descriptions for your pins. These are two different ways that you can tie a keyword with your image in order to have it displayed when someone is looking for specific pins.

Hashtags

A hashtag (#) or sometimes called the pound sign, is a symbol that you can use when writing your descriptions that will tell Pinterest that the word following the symbol is important and a keyword. For example, if you tag an image of a cat with #cat, Pinterest knows that the image is relevant to the word cat. So when someone searches for cat on Pinterest, your image will be included in the results.

The hashtag is used quite often on Twitter and has become commonplace for a lot of social networking sites to be used to identify keywords. You will see it used quite often in advertising in relation to Twitter.

Mentions

Mentions (@) are adapted from their use on Twitter and are used to include the original person or source on a message, so that they are sent a copy of the tweet. In Pinterest, when you include a mention, it will notify that individual that you mentioned them in a pin.

To create a mention, just include the users name with the @ symbol in the beginning. For example, to mention me in a description, type @IngeniousIncome. I will be sent a notification that you did this. This is a great way to gain followers and let other people know you are interested in the same things that they are.

Adding a Hashtag to a Pin

As mentioned above, to add a hashtag to a pin, just include a # symbol before any important keywords in your description. For an example, suppose we had a pin of a puppy next to a Christmas tree. Our description might read as follows:

A cute #puppy next to a beautiful #Christmas tree.

We've told Pinterest that the keywords puppy and Christmas are important in this description and that they are keywords. Notice though, that because there is a space between Christmas and tree, it doesn't identify both of those keywords together. In order to hashtag those together you would either have to add a hyphen (#Christmas-tree) or place the words together (#Christmastree). A third way to do it would be to add a hashtag individually (#Christmas #tree), however if anyone searches for the word Tree by itself, your image could be displayed as a result. You'll have to use your best judgement. In the image below, I've added a few hashtags.

Now I should state that if you don't add a hashtag it doesn't mean that your keyword will not be displayed. It's very possible it will be displayed without the inclusion of the tag. However, by adding in the hashtag, you are helping Pinterest better understand your pin so that it can properly identify what it is.

Additionally, when you add a hashtag to a keyword, you are making that keyword a clickable link in your description. So with a keyword like #mantle, the word mantle can now be clicked on and it will search Pinterest for that keyword, in this case mantle.

Searching for Pins with Hashtags

You can use hashtags to your advantage when you are searching for pins on Pinterest. If you enter a hashtag (#) with a keyword, such as #mantle, you will be shown all the pins that have #mantle in their descriptions. You will also get pins that have the keyword mantle included in their description.

Also when you find a pin that has a hashtag in its description, you can click on the keyword after the # symbol to search for that word on Pinterest. This will make it easier to find similar pins.

Chapter 8: Viewing and Editing Your Pinterest Activity

As you start working with your Pinterest account, it is possible to lose track of your pins or your boards. Thankfully there are a few easy ways to view what you've pinned and liked, so that you can find those boots you thought were so cute, but forgot to add them to a board.

Viewing Your Pinterest Activity

All your activity on Pinterest is saved in your Activity area on your profile. You can access this area, by clicking on your **Name** to bring up your Profile account. Once you have your account up, on the tool bar next to the Edit Profile button is the word Activity. Click on **Activity** to display your activity starting with the most recent changes and additions. This information is limited to the last pins you created and only goes back a little ways. It is limited on how much you can see through this view.

Viewing Your Boards

To view your pinboards, you can either click on your name or hover over your name and click on **Boards** on the menu. This will bring up all the boards you have created. The boards will list how many pins are in each board and will display a preview of the last 4 pins that were added and the cover image for the board.

If you are on another page in your profile, you can click on the menu item that lists the number of boards you have, such as 32 boards, to bring you back to the board page.

Viewing Your Pins

To view your pins, without any filtering by boards, just click on the menu item that lists the number of pins you have, such as 245 pins, to take you to the pin page.

Viewing Your Likes

If you have liked any pins, you can display those likes on a single page by clicking on the menu item that lists the number of likes you have , such as 114 likes, to take you to the likes page. Just a reminder, you can like a pin without adding it to a pinboard. This is a great way to keep a pin for review at a later time without having to add it to one of your boards.

Editing and Deleting Pins on a Pinboard

If you want to make changes to any of your pins, you can do that by hovering over the pin and clicking on the **Edit** button. On the Edit page, you can change the description, the URL that the image links to or the board that it's located on. Once you make any changes, click **Save Pin** to commit those changes.

If you change your mind about adding a particular pin or you added multiple copies of a pin, you can delete the pin from your board. To do this, hover over the image and click on the **Edit** button when it appears.

On the edit page, click on the **Delete Pin** button located on the right side. A confirmation window will appear giving you chance to cancel the action before the image is removed.

Note: When deleting a pin, it will be removed from your account permanently. You cannot keep pins on your account without them being located on a board. If you don't want to delete the pin completely, some people setup an alternate board named something like Temporary or Under Review to place those images in. You can also click on Like for that image and then you will be able to find the image again by reviewing your Likes.

Chapter 9: Sharing Pins to Facebook and Twitter

Sharing Pins Via Facebook

Sharing pins via Facebook is easy to do, especially if you already linked your Pinterest account with your Facebook account when you created your account. Let's look at your settings to make sure it's setup properly. I highly recommend you at least check these settings. I found that I prefer having the settings adjusted so that Pinterest wasn't spamming my Facebook account.

First click on your name and select **Settings** to open your profile page. Scroll down just a little ways and you will find the Facebook On-Off switch. Right next to this is an option to **Link To Facebook**, if you haven't already. If you have, already linked your account with Facebook, it will say Login with Facebook.

If you have not linked your account, when you click on this link a Facebook Pinterest app window will come up. Click **Go To App**

to continue. Once this window goes away you can then choose if you wish to have Pinterest automatically post your pinning activity to your Facebook timeline. I personally chose not to enable this option. It created way too many posts so I disabled it, but you may prefer to have it enabled. I recommend you test it out and see what works best for you.

Once you turn Publish activity to Facebook Timeline on, a new window appears from Facebook asking you to Add to Facebook, the Pinterest connectivity. Once this window disappears, click on **Save Profile** to complete the process.

One item to note is that currently you can only link to a personal Facebook account and not business pages. This may change in the future with the new business Pinterest accounts.

I've have had a few people who have enabled this feature to post to your Facebook Timeline account and it doesn't appear to be working. I've found that if you turn off the Add Pinterest to Facebook Timeline and then turn it back on, it will often resolve the issue. Just be sure to click **Save Settings** as you turn it off and then again when you turn it back on.

If you are still having problems having your pins show up on Facebook, you might have to adjust the settings for Pinterest on Facebook. To do this, go to www.facebook.com/settings?tab=applications and then click on Apps on the left sidebar. Next to Pinterest, click on Edit and then look at the option next to Posts on your behalf. Make sure that Everyone, Friends or some other group is selected.

Sharing single pins and boards on Facebook

You can Like a particular pin or a board right inside Pinterest. To do this, click on the board or the pin you want to Like on Facebook. On the right side of the page, you'll find a Facebook Like button.

When you add a new pin to one of your boards, you will have an option where you can check a box to automatically share your new pin on Facebook.

Sharing Pins Via Twitter

You can also link your Pinterest account to your Twitter account and then tweet your pins right from inside Pinterest. Linking the accounts is just as easy as it was to link your Facebook account. Just click on your name and select Settings from the drop-down menu. Your Edit Profile page will come up. Scroll down just past the Facebook linking area and you will see where you can link your Twitter account. As with the Facebook linking process, click on Login with Twitter. A new window will open asking you to authorize Pinterest to link to your Twitter account. If you aren't already signed into Twitter, you will have to do so to continue. Once that's completed, the window will close. Click on Save Profile to complete the process.

Twitter integration is a little different from Facebook, in that you don't have to manage the posting through the setting page. When you create a new pin now that you have your Twitter account linked to your Pinterest account, you will now have an option to have your pin posted on Twitter automatically. It doesn't do it without your permission for each pin.

One question I have often received is, if I signed up for Pinterest with my Facebook account or email, can I connect with Twitter too? The answer is yes, you can connect both Facebook and Twitter to your account without any confusion or complications. Pinterest is rather unique in being able to work well with both social media services.

Sharing Pins On Twitter

Now that you've linked your Pinterest account with Twitter, you have two ways to share pins from your Pinterest account. Just like Facebook, on each individual pin you do have a button you can click on the right side of the page to "Tweet" the pin. When you click this button, a new window will appear with the description of the pin and a link to it already typed into a box. You can edit the text in the box, but it's best to leave the link as it is. This link lets someone click on the tweet to view your pin on Pinterest. Once you've made any changes you want to make, click on Tweet. You're pin will be shared on your Twitter feed and the box will close.

When you create a new pin, you will also have the option to check a box to add your new pin to your Twitter feed. Just check the box and finish adding your pin. If you have both Facebook and Twitter linked to your Pinterest account, you will have check boxes that will allow you to add your pin to both services at the same time.

Sharing Pins with non-Pinterest users via email

There are many people who have not yet discovered Pinterest. If you want to gain further exposure to your Pinterest account, you can include a link to your Pinterest account in your emails. Some people add a link to their boards in their email signature. Depending on which email service you use, editing your signature can be different. I won't go into how to do that, however if you want to link to your Pinterest account in your email, just use the following URL. **http://www.pinterest.com/username**. You can identify your user name on your Settings page, by clicking on your name and then on Settings.

Linking to a Pinterest board via email

What if you just want to send a link for one of your boards to a family member or friend. Each board has it's own URL (**http://www.pinterest.com/username/boardname/**) . The quick and easy way to get this URL is to open the board in your web-browser and then copy and paste the URL that appears in your browser's address bar.

Chapter 10: Protecting Yourself

Inevitably, a service like Pinterest can be a nuisance just as easily as it can be beneficial. But knowing how to manage different features on the site will help protect you and make the experience as enjoyable as possible.

Adjusting Pinterest Settings

We've touched on this before in various places throughout this book, but I felt it best to include it here as well. If you hover over your name and then select **Settings**, you will be taken to the Edit Account Settings page. Here is where most of the important settings are controlled. Some of the more useful settings are where you have the ability to link to your Facebook account, control how Pinterest posts to your Facebook Timeline, link to your Twitter account and where you can hide your profile from the search engines.

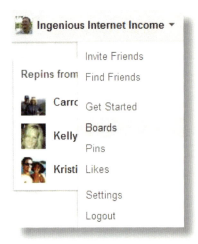

Unlink Your Twitter Account

If you wish to unlink your Twitter account, you can do it even if you are using your Twitter account to log into your Pinterest account. On the Edit Account Settings page, scroll down to the Twitter option, and turn the connection to **Off**. Save your profile and your changes are saved.

Unlink Your Facebook Account

You can adjust the connection to your Facebook account either completely or just in part easily. Again, go to your Edit Account Settings page and scroll down to the Facebook section.

If you wish to stop the link to Facebook, change the Add Pinterest To Facebook Timeline setting to Off and click Save Profile. This will disable the automatic posting to your Facebook Timeline page.

If you wish to completely remove the connection to Facebook, click the Login with Facebook On button. This will bring up a new window that will ask for your Facebook password. Enter your password in the box and press Disconnect Facebook. The switch will change back to Off. Click on Save Profile to save your changes.

If you wish to reconnect either of these accounts at a future time, you will have to go through the process of adding the accounts back to your Pinterest account.

Reporting Spam Pins

Even Pinterest isn't free from spam. One of the ways this appears on Pinterest is when you click on a pins image and instead of being taken to the original image source, you're redirected to a survey or an advertisement. One of the great features of Pinterest is giving the users the ability to help manage the content on the site. Simply click the back button to come back to the pin and then click on the Report button on the right side of the screen. You'll have a new window come up asking you why you are reporting this pin.

Choose the spam option and then click Report Pin at the bottom of the window. At this point you should see a confirmation window and then it will come back to the original pin page.

Pinterest will review the report and remove the pin if it violates the Terms of Use. If Pinterest receives numerous reports about a particular user, that account could be suspended.

Change Your Password

As always, your password is the only thing keeping other's from compromising your account. I highly recommend that you use a password that isn't easily guessed or figured out. It's also recommended to change your password periodically. There are currently no specific requirements for what you use for your password on Pinterest.

If you find that you need to change your password at any point, you can do this on the Edit Account Settings page. Scroll down on that page, until you see the button labeled **Change Password**. Click on this button to open the change password process. You will first have to enter you current password and then enter a new password twice before clicking on **Change Password**. Once the changes have been saved you will be returned to your Profile page.

Give Credit To The Original Image Creator

One of the biggest concerns that was brought up when Pinterest began, was the question about the legality of sharing images on the site. There are still many questions around this topic that haven't been completely answered, but to protect yourself, be sure to always link back to the original source of any image you pin to Pinterest.

By being sure to give credit to the original source of the image, you are complying with the Pinterest Terms of Service and you'll letting the original owner know that you are doing your best to give credit to the original source. The best way to completely protect yourself is to either post only original content that you created or to pin images by using the Pin It button from the original sources website, if they have provided one.

Blocking Pin It Use For Your Website

What if you want to completely prevent anyone from pinning images from your website? Is there anyway to do this? There is a way provided by Pinterest to do this.

Blocking Pin It Sitewide

To block pins from your entire website, you can do this two different ways. The first is to submit a request to Pinterest to block access to any images on your site. Visit **https://pinterest.com/ about/copyright/block/** to submit a request. At the time this book was written, this was in beta testing and there is a chance that this option has changed.

The other way to do this is by adding a line of code to the header of your website. If you add the following code between the opening <head> tag and the closing </head> tag, it will prevent anyone from pinning images from your site. When someone tries to pin an image, they will be shown a message saying that pinning is not allowed. The code is as follows:

<meta name="pinterest" content="nopin" />

Blocking Pin It on a single image

If you have a single image you want to block from being able to be pinned, you can add a single attribute to the image. In your code editor find the line that starts with <img for the image you want to protect. At the end of that line of code, right before the closing /> tag, add the following attribute nopin = "nopin". You're line should look like the following once completed.

<img src="http://www.yoursite.com/picture.jpg" nopin="nopin" />

Reporting Copyright Infringement

If you find an image that you own the copyright to on Pinterest and want the image removed, Pinterest provides a form that makes this process easy to complete. To report an image, copy the URL of the pinned image. Then visit the following website to register a request. **http://www.pinterest.com/about/copyright**. Read the provided information and then click on Copyright Complaint Form. Be sure to completely fill out the form provided and include the link to the pin then click on the button, **Submit notification** once you're finished.

Reporting Trademark Infringement

If you find out that someone is using your trademark in a way that you don't want, you can submit a request just like you can for copyright issues. The form can be found here: **http://www.pinterest.com/about/trademark/form**. You will need the username in question and details about the trademark including the registration number. Click on Submit when you are finished.

Conclusion

Pinterest is a wonderful site to express yourself and to have some fun. It's also turning into a great way to market your business and to gain new customers. As a fairly new social media site, it's constantly evolving. More and more new features are being added all the time.

In order to keep up with the most recent changes and features, be sure to visit my site where I am adding new information all the time.

It's my desire to teach you how to get the most from Pinterest in an easy to understand format. In order for me to know how best to do this, please email me any comments or questions you might have about Pinterest. I'd be more than happy to answer.

I have another guide available that you might be interested in. It's **The Ingenious Guide To Twitter**, which can be found on Amazon.com

Need Help?

I am constantly adding new training articles and information on my site and I'd be more than happy to help you should you need it. Either contact me via email at steve@ingeniousinternetincome.com or visit my site - **www.ingeniousinternetincome.com**.

Questions or Comments?

I'd love to hear your thoughts. Email me at: **steve@ ingeniousinternetincome.com**

You can find my Pinterest account at **http://www.pinterest.com/ IngeniousIncome**

You can follow me on Twitter at **http://www.twitter.com/ IngeniousIncome**

And be sure to Like my Facebook page at **http://www.facebook. com/IngeniousInternetIncomeWithSteveEason**

One Last Thing ...

If you enjoyed this book and believe the book is worth sharing, would you take a few seconds to let your friends know about it? I am sure that they would be forever grateful to you. As will I.

Steve Eason
Ingenious Internet Income

Made in the USA
Lexington, KY
23 September 2013